QUEEN OF THE WITCHES
OR WISE CRONE

JOY REICHARD, M.A.

FROM PART III OF THE BOOK

CELEBRATE THE DIVINE FEMININE

RECLAIM YOU POWER WITH ANCIENT GODDESS WISDOM

The information in this book is provided for informational purposes only and is not a substitute for professional advice. The author and publisher make no legal claims, express or implied, and the material is not intended to replace the services of a physician, psychologist, therapist, counselor, or other qualified professional.

The author, publisher, and/or copyright holder assume no responsibility for the loss or damage caused, or allegedly caused, directly or indirectly by the use of information contained in this book. The author and publisher specifically disclaim any liability incurred from the use or application of the contents of this book.

In order to respect their privacy, names and identifying characteristics of clients and people described in this book have been changed.

The publisher does not have any control over and does not assume any responsibility for author or third-party websites and their content.

Cover Art: Krystal Jenson

All photos were taken by author unless otherwise indicated.

Many thanks to Shannon Dawn for her contribution of the Hecate Ritual.

Visit the author website: http://joyreichard.com or http:celebratedivinefeminine.com

The publisher does not have any control over and does not assume any responsibility for author or third-party websites and their content.

HECATE

QUEEN OF THE WITCHES OR WISE CRONE

Triple-faced Hecate is one of the most ancient images of pre-Hellenic mythology. In this section you will learn about Hecate's geographical and historical origins. Even though Hecate has ties to the ancient Mother Goddess you will come to understand how over time she became allied with the archetype of the crone, was relegated of the underworld and came to be associated with death and witch craft. You will also learn how her connection to the underworld also links her to the psychological realm of the subconscious and to transformation and change. Hecate can be a helpful guide when you must journey into the depths of your subconscious to reflect and re-evaluate your life. Her transformative powers can help you release what no longer serves you so you can make room for new opportunities and growth.

Hecate reminds us of the value of the crone, the wise elder who offers wisdom and insight. She provides a powerful model to emulate for those of us who have reached their crone hood. On my 60th birthday I threw myself a party and invited my women friends, many who are still my sisters in the goddess. We had a joyous celebration of my wise crone status. I have had my years of struggle and pain, and felt I needed to celebrate the wisdom I acquired earning those winkles and grey hair! I highly recommend a similar celebration for any of you who have attained this auspicious phase of your life.

In the guided visualization you will have an opportunity to join Hecate and a group of her devotees around a bubbling cauldron on a moonlit night. You will be invited to join them in releasing what no longer serves you, so you can call in new energies for personal growth and expansion. The ritual is an extension of this visualization as you cycle through three altars to discard the old, call upon Hecate for guidance, and breathe life into new ideas and goals.

Hecate's nature and roles have shifted greatly over the centuries and sometimes seem almost contradictory. She has been worshipped as the Great Mother, as well as the Crone. She has been linked to the moon, is guardian of the crossroad and is said to preside over magic, ritual, prophetic vision, childbirth, death, the underworld, and the secrets of regeneration. During the Middle Ages Hecate became associated with black magic and was debased as the hag, or Queen of the Witches, who led satanic rites.

Hecate is one of the oldest primordial figures and is pre-Olympian. She can be linked back to the ancient frog-headed Egyptian goddess Heket. As mid-wife it was said that Heket help to birth the sun every morning. Heket evolved into Heq, the tribal matriarch of pre-dynastic Egypt.

According to some traditions Hecate's geographic origin was Thrace, a part of present day Greece and Bulgaria. She was an ancient and powerful Thracian divinity, and a Titan, who ruled heaven, earth and the sea. She was said to bestow wealth, victory, wisdom, and good luck on mortals. If, however, she felt a mortal was unworthy, she could also withhold her blessings. It is said that she assisted the gods in the war with the Gigantes, and slew the giant Clytius.

When I was in Bulgaria in 2004, I visited a 1200 BCE Thracian tomb which contained murals of a king foretelling his life in the afterworld. He would rule as king and be honored by the goddess Hecate, or Bendies as she was sometimes called. The goddess was shown welcoming the king to the underworld with the sacred  pomegranate. When the king died, his favorite wife was sacrificed so that she might also accompany him to the underworld. This is not an honor that you or I would appreciate today!

Other sources claim that Hecate was worshipped from middle and southern Europe to Anatolia as far back as 5000 to 6000 years ago, to pre-patriarchal times. The indigenous Neolithic inhabitants of Old Europe, Anatolia and Northern Africa, which dates back some 9000 years ago, were thought to be matrilineal, matrifocal, agrarian, and peace-loving.

They worshipped a mother goddess who presided over the cycles of life – birth, death and rebirth.

Along the Danube in Eastern Europe the frog goddess was a symbol of fertility, death, rebirth and transformation. Patriarchal influences began to overtake the Neolithic Mother Goddess cultures around approximately 5000 years ago. About that time sky god worshipping semi-nomadic invaders from the eastern steppes of Russia who were hierarchical, patriarchal, and aggressive began to migrate into the region.

This ancient Mother Goddess preceded Hecate, and quite possibly evolved into Hecate. As patriarchy took root and male gods became more dominant, the goddesses became more submissive and less powerful. Many of Hecate's attributes were split off and given to other goddesses such as Demeter, Persephone and Artemis. Hecate was relegated to her underworld qualities and lost much of her prominence.

Hecate was worshipped by the Amazons who were mother goddess worshipping matrifocal and matrilineal nomadic tribes that lived in Anatolia and North Africa near the Black Sea. The Amazons were believed to have founded several cities in Anatolia (Turkey) and were the first to tame horses. The most famous princess and priestess of Hecate was the sorceress, Medea, who resided in Colchis which is located on the eastern end of Black Sea in Anatolia. It is noted for being Amazon country. There is a statue of Medea in Colchis. This area, according to a friend of mine who spent several years in the country of Georgia, is still known for its strong women.

Hecate appears in the ancient texts of the Eleusinian Mysteries of pre-Hellenic Greece. These ancient mysteries involve a descent into the underworld that is somewhat similar to the descent myths of both Inanna and Dumuzi, and Isis and Osiris. In this myth Persephone, the beloved daughter of Demeter, is abducted by Hades, the dreaded Lord of the Underworld. She is carried off to his kingdom. It is Hecate who witnesses Persephone's abduction, and who also greets Persephone upon her return. In pre-Hellenic Greece it was believed that Hecate resided in the underworld as its queen and was the guardian of the souls.

In Classical Greek Mythology Hecate was the daughter of Titans: Perses, the Titan god of destruction, and Asteria, a star goddess. Asteria was a sister of Leto, the mother of Apollo and Artemis. Hecate was, therefore, the cousin of Artemis. Hecate was respected by Zeus, and was the only deity aside from Zeus who had the power to grant or withhold anything she wanted from humans.

Hecate was worshiped as a moon goddess - the dark aspect of the moon. She was the mirror image of her cousin, Artemis, who was the light aspect of the moon. Selene was the aspect of the full moon. This dark aspect links Hecate to Isis of Egypt, as well as the Black Madonna in Europe. Interestingly it is the dark goddesses who are most strongly connected to healing powers and the dark moon. The shrines of the Black Virgins/Madonnas of Europe are frequently connected to miracles and healing powers. They are often attributed to having more powers than those Virgins of the white aspects.

Hecate, as the great Triple Goddess -- or Hecate Triformis -- is a form of the original trinity: maiden, mother, and aging wise woman or crone. The Virgin was Kore/Persephone, Ceres or Demeter was the Mother, and the crone, or wise woman, was Hecate. Hecate was also part of the three phases of woman's mating relationships: Hebe as maiden, Hera the wife and Hecate as the widow. In women's agricultural mysteries her trinity took the form of Kore as the green corn; Persephone as the ripe ear; and Hecate as the harvested corn. As the Christian trinity postdates the Triple Goddess, it probably evolved from this original goddess trinity, with the wisdom of the crone, or Hecate, going to the Holy Spirit.

When I visited the Thracian tomb while traveling in Bulgaria, our groups was quite excited to notice that painted on the dome ceiling was a Thracian representation of the seven levels of heaven. There were three charioteers driving the heavens or the cosmos. (see image above, "Reproduction of Thracian tomb 2". Licensed under CC BY-SA 3.0 via Commons - https://commons.wikimedia.org/wiki/File:Reproducti on_of_Thracian_tomb_2.jpg#/media/).

Upon closer inspection we noticed that not only were the charioteers women, but in fact it was the Triple Goddess as Maiden, Mother, and Crone who was driving the heavens! To reiterate, this tomb predated Christ by over 1200 years!

There is a famous pillar called the Hectaerion which depicts the three aspects of Hecate. The three females represent Hecate's powers over heaven, earth and underworld as well as her control over birth, life and death. Their six arms carry three torches, a key, a rope and a dagger. The key illustrates her role as guardian of the deep mysteries; only Hecate possesses the key that unlocks them. The rope possibly symbolizes the umbilical cord, or represents her role of bringing souls into the underworld and helping them to be reborn. The dagger symbolizes cutting through illusions to true power. The dagger later becomes the *athame* of Wicca.

The aspect for which Hecate is most honored is that of the crone. As the wise woman Hecate offers words of wisdom and provides valuable counsel as well as protection. An ancient ritual honoring Hecate involved leaving food at crossroads where three paths meet. It was called Hecate's Supper. This ritual food was left when important decisions had to be made. The supplicants asked for guidance and the most favorable outcome. In life we often find that the way is not clear and confusion exists. This is especially true in today's troubled times. Hecate is the goddess of wisdom and vision. She sees the past, present and future and can be called upon to help us make wise decisions and good choices.

Hecate's responsibility as guardian of souls degenerated over time as patriarchy became more entrenched and the status of goddesses continued to deteriorate. Eventually Hecate became a shadowy haunting hag-like figure that at night sent out demons and phantoms who taught sorcery and witchcraft. These underworld beings were said to dwell where two roads crossed, at tombs, and near the blood of murdered persons. Hecate wandered with the souls of the dead; her approach was announced by the whining and howling of dogs.

The realm of the underworld over which Hecate rules has not always been viewed as a place of punishment. It was the Christians who invented the concept of Hell as a place of unending torture. Originally the underworld was the place of the dead. It was a stopover place while the dead prepared for rebirth. Hecate, as you remember, witnessed both Persephone's descent into the underworld and her return. By being both behind and in front of Persephone, Hecate is symbolically protecting and guiding her. It also symbolized her role as the Queen of the Underworld. Hecate was viewed by the ancient Greeks as the Mistress of Souls who lighted the way as she conveyed souls to the underworld at death. She also guided them on their return when it was time for them to be reborn. In our Western culture death is a taboo subject. Our elderly are shown little respect, thought to be senile or out of touch, and are hidden away in senior residences.

How are the elders treated in your own family? In your community?

Our culture favors youth and has an aversion to aging. Take time to notice the numerous commercials and advertisements on beauty products. Notice how many of the actors and models are young and attractive. Only recently with the aging of the Baby Boomers have mature middle aged women begun to make an appearance on commercials, and most of those are for health related products. Hecate is the confident wise Crone who appreciates the knowledge gained from a life of experiences, relationships and lessons. She knows death and does not fear it because death is only a transition leading to renewal and rebirth.

The ancients had no concept of an inner or psychological realm. The inner world was the spirit realm where all the spirits dwelt. Even today our inner creative world can seem mysterious and appears to be filled with surprises. Hecate is the guardian of the crossroads of our unconscious, the hidden part of our psyches which is the source of our creativity, growth and healing. Sometimes gaining wisdom requires a descent into the underworld of our subconscious where inspiration and vision, the creative juices of renewal, are often found. Because Western culture emphasizes action and productivity, it frequently devalues those times of deep introspection. We have been conditioned to experience them as being stuck, in limbo, or as being depressed. In reality these spaces of non-activity may be part of the journey to revitalization. Hecate, if invited, acts as our guide in this deep inner work.

In my practice I frequently have clients who

exhibit symptoms of depression. Many report that their doctors would automatically give them anti-depressants rather than taking time to delve into the source of their low moods. I agree that for the clinically depressed anti-depressants are often warranted and necessary, and can be beneficial to a person's quality of life. However, I have found, at least for many of my clients, that what they needed was someone to listen to them. They needed an objective and caring ear to help them sort through the confusion of their concerns, while providing encouragement and tools to help them shift towards a more positive attitude. Going inward can be a productive time of deep reflection that can result in growth and change. Being too quick to take a pill can deprive a person of a valuable opportunity to arrive at important insights and self-realizations.

Transformation and change often requires releasing what no longer serves us. We humans often fear letting go of old beliefs, relationships, assumptions and perceptions about life, as well as letting go of our physical body. We protest and struggle, trying to hold onto the familiar, even though it might be the source of our pain. I have experienced clients with 50 pounds or more to lose crying with frustration and shame over their weight. Yet they were reluctant to adhere to a food plan or exercise routine. I've had other clients who were in painfully dysfunctional and abusive relationships that are desperate for change, yet are terrified to let go.

We must face the emptiness and fear of the unknown if we are to receive Hecate's gift of vision and renewal. We must face the Dark Goddess. We can surrender to Hecate what needs to be released so we can be reborn. Many times, even though we protest, the Crone will claim us and recycle us through her cauldron despite our struggles and cries of resistance. Maybe you have already had this experience!

Hecate was skilled in the arts of divining and foretelling the future. As she looks three ways at once, Hecate gives us an expanded vision whereby we can see the present, or warnings or promises of the future, or recall teachings or learnings from the past. She gives us dreams and prophetic visions, whispers secrets into our inner ears, and enables us to converse with the spirits of the dead and our guides. As Queen of Ghosts, Mother of Witches, Mistress of Magic, Hecate bestows magical knowledge. She was said to hold the secrets of magical spells, charms, enchantments, and the medicinal use of both healing and destructive substances. One of Hecate's rituals took place on moonless nights at a three-fold crossroads. In a sacred cauldron special herbs were mixed with wine, milk or blood and boiled while Hecate was invoked. Sacred cauldrons also appear in other mythologies from around the world including Hindu, Norse, Babylonian, Chaldean and Hittite myths.

Late in the1400 CE, an inquisition was unleashed to hunt, torture and burn witches. It lasted until the 1600's, a period during which nine million witches, 80% women including young girls, were exterminated. This was a period of asceticism in which the church denigrated anything of the flesh and had a misogynistic hatred of all that brought life into the world. Anyone could accuse a witch, and the accused were considered guilty until proven innocent. They were frequently tortured for confessions and to implicate others until a coven of thirteen was identified. It is believed that few of those convicted really belonged to a coven or were truly witches. The victims were the elderly, senile, mentally ill, handicapped, physically unappealing, the village beauties that incited lust, homosexuals or freethinkers. It was the midwives, healers and seers, those who did the most good for the country people, who were identified by the Church as the most dangerous.

Instead of valuing and honoring these women for the healers they were, and for the wisdom and knowledge they brought to the community, these women were burned at the stake or hanged as witches. There were accused of being inhabited by evil spirits such as Hecate. A video by Starhawk called *Burning Times* is a thought provoking documentary about the witch hunts and trials during this period. I recommend it for those who want more information about this period in our history.

Hecate was demonized by the Catholic authorities. They projected onto her their fears and insecurities of the powerful dark feminine. They distorted her into an ugly Queen of Witches. Many pagan country people persisted in practicing their ancient fertility rites and folk customs. This angered and horrified the Church. Because the patriarchal authorities could not control Hecate; and because they didn't understand the powers of the dark feminine, they demonized her. They taught fear of this goddess envisioned as a twisted old hag, who, like the dark of the moon, was considered to be negative and even hostile to men. It was said that she stalked the crossroads at night with her vicious hounds of hell waiting to snatch unsuspecting wayfarers to her land of the dead. They portrayed her as the moon goddess of ghosts and the dead surrounded by a swarm of female demons. And as Queen of Ghosts she was believed to fly through the night, followed by a dreadful train of ghoulish spirits and baying hounds. She was said to give her priestesses the power to enchant, to turn men into animals, and to smite them with madness.

Realizing how Hecate has been maligned by Western religious authorities, it is important to reclaim her for who she truly is:

- ➢ The wise crone who is protectress, guardian, and counselor.
- ➢ Guardian of the Crossroads who offers wisdom, guidance and counsel when important decisions need to be made.
- ➢ Queen of the Underworld, who offers hope for fertility, renewal, and regeneration.
- ➢ Light Bearer, Guardian of the Souls, who protects and offers guidance as she guides souls to the underworld.
- ➢ Guardian of the Unconscious, of transitions, who guards the doorways of birth, death and transformation
- ➢ Mistress of Magic and Divination

In summary, it is important to remember that with the advent of patriarchy the power and prestige of women and the goddess declined, and with that Hecate's status. She was demoted to a shadowy hag-like figure who allied with ghosts and evil spirits. She was further demeaned under the auspices of the Catholic Church who conceptualized the underworld as a hellish place and came to associate Hecate, who was the Queen of the Underworld, as the Queen of Witches.

In reality Hecate, who has links to the ancient Neolithic Mother Goddess, is a revered ancient mother archetype who is also frequently imaged as the archetype of the wise crone. Hecate reminds us that wisdom comes from life's experiences. Our female elders, the crones, are valuable repositories of insight and information that can help us navigate through our own personal challenges.

If you are a "crone," then Hecate provides a powerful model of strength and wisdom to emulate. With her ability to see the past, present, and future, she is a symbol of wisdom who can be sought for guidance and assistance when difficult decisions need to be made. Because she sees clearly, Hecate also knows when it is time to remove the debris from our lives so we can make room for new opportunities. Hecate is a goddess who is worthy of honor and respect.

HECATE DISCUSSION QUESTIONS

• What season of a women's life do your fall into - Maiden, Mother or Crone. What do you like about this time in your life? What do you dislike?

• How does our culture view the crone, the image of the old woman?

• If we as a culture honored the expanded version of the crone, how might that change our culture?

• Have you experienced the underworld in the form of grief, abandonment, loss, rejection, etc.? Describe what you learned from this experience.

• How have you dealt with times of transition, crisis, or indecision in the past? How might invoking Hecate as a guide and torch bearer help you light the way?

HECATE SOURCES AND RECOMMENDED READINGS

D. J. Conway, *Maiden, Mother, Crone: the Myth and Reality of the Triple Goddess*.

Elizabeth Fisher, *Rise Up and Call Her Name: A Woman-honoring Journey into Global Earth-based Spiritualities*.

Demetra George, *Mysteries of the Dark Moon: The Healing Power of the Dark Goddess*.

Marija Gimbutas, *The Language of the Goddess*.

Merlin Stone, *Ancient Mirrors of Womanhood: a Treasury of Goddess and Heroine Lore from Around the World*.

Barbara G. Walker, *The Women's Encyclopedia of Myths and Secrets*.

Hekate: http://hekate.timerift.net/roles.htm.

Theoi Greek Mythology, Hecate: http://www.theoi.com/Khthonios/Hecate.html

Hecate: http://en.wikipedia.org/wiki/Hecate.

HECATE GUIDED VISUALIZATION

Music Suggestion: "Transformation" – *Return* by Sophia, Chakra Healing Zone

Pass out pens and small slips of paper before the meditation.

Close your eyes and take a nice deep breath and as you slowly exhale begin to release all the tension and stress of the day..... Take another deep breath, breathing into your abdomen, and hold... and release slowly, just letting go of all your worries and cares. ..... And now take a third deep breath and as you exhale just surrender to total peace and relaxation...... Now that you are cleansed of stress and worry and cares, begin to call back to yourself all the pieces you may have scattered about over the past days and weeks. Just call all those pieces back and let them spiral right back into your heart space and feel yourself becoming even more centered and calm....

And now let's count backwards from 10 to 1 and with each number imagine that you are descending a staircase, a staircase that leads through time and space to another place, another era. 10, going deeper now, 9, 8, 7... 6... 5... 4... 3... 2... 1...

Now you find yourself on a moonlit road walking through a forest. There is a full moon shining through the tall pines, throwing moon shadows on the ground. The evening is peaceful, and you feel safe, though you are walking with a heavy burden, a heavy load that you have been carrying for a long time. Maybe it is a decision that weighs heavy on your mind, or a challenge or situation that is tugging at your heart. Or maybe it is a something, a belief, attitude, or behavior that you are struggling to release, but just can't seem to let it go. You know what it is........ As you walk you hear a sound: a sound of chanting, of women's voices raised in song. You walk towards the singing until you come to a crossroads where three roads meet. Women are gathered there in a circle chanting and swaying to the music. They have gathered around a bonfire upon which rests a huge cauldron. The cauldron emits the comforting smell of herbs and spices.

The women in the circle hear your approach and turn to greet you. They welcome you into their circle. There is an old woman standing at the cauldron. She gently stirs the bubbling mixture uttering chants as she stirs. She looks up at you and nods a beautiful smile in welcome inviting you to join the circle. This is the cauldron of release and transformation, you are told. The women have gathered to release and transform that which no longer serves them. They are here to release and cleanse and be renewed. A time of change, transition, and new possibilities lies ahead. They are here to regenerate and prepare themselves.

Now the ritual is about to begin. The women, some sitting, some standing, all become quiet and deeply reflective. They are reflecting on what they are wanting to release. Then one by one the women move up to the cauldron and toss in that which they are ready to let go. For one it is her jealousy that is poisoning her relationships. For another it is the need to control others. For another it is the lack of clarity about an issue she needs to resolve. She is seeking to release doubt and indecision.

Now it is your turn. You get up and approach the cauldron and prepare to release the old so you can make room for the new. What is it that you want to release... (pause)

When every woman is done, Hecate stops stirring the cauldron. She utters incantations and makes hand signs imparting the magic of release and transformation.

Then she begins to move from woman to woman looking deep into each woman's eyes. She asks each woman what it is they need or want from the great wise crone, the dark goddess of transformation, tonight......

Then it is your turn. You look into her face which is a mass of lines and winkles from eons of experience. Her eyes are deep pools of compassion, wisdom, and unconditional love. Her gaze pierces deep into your soul and unlocks that deepest part of you. You begin to feel a swirl of energy as you tell her what you desire -- what you need from Hecate tonight... (pause for 30 seconds)

When Hecate finally completes speaking with all the women gathered in the circle, you see that all the requests have become a huge swirl of energy. She walks back to the fire and with more incantations of magic she flings her arms upwards over the fire so the desires and dreams and requests can be carried up to the heavens with the smoke to be manifested. You feel the energies as they swirl upwards to be received by the All That Is.

After a time the energies begin to calm. Hecate turns and smiles saying that the magic has been set in motion. Now it is time to celebrate the manifestation of intentions and dreams. Someone brings out a flute, another a drum, another a zither, and so on -- and the music begins. Then, as some women starts to sing … others begin to sway... and then to dance to the familiar chants. Soon all the women are celebrating -- dancing under the light of the moon, warmed by the fire and each other's company.

Finally it is time to leave. You take your leave of the new friends you have made and begin walking back through the forest. Though it is late and the forest is quiet, you feel safe, at peace and deeply contented. You feel as if a deep inner change has taken place, and you have a sense of quiet expectation for the future.

Now you return to the staircase and begin to climb upward to this time and this place. 1 2 3 4 5 6 7 8 9 10. Come back feeling the breath in your lungs, the weight of your body in the chair, feel your feet upon the floor, and when you are ready, take a deep breath, stretch and open your eyes.

Reflections after the Meditation

As you come back, please take a few minutes to write down your experience on the paper provided.

On the smaller slips of paper write down what you were ready to release. This will be used in our ritual tonight.

(An audio recording of this guided visualization may be purchased on my website at

www.celebratedivinefeminine.com .

HECATE RITUAL

By Shannon Dawn

Music Suggestion: "Hecate" – *The Year is a Dancing Woman*, Vol. 2 by Ruth Barrett

***Pass out pen and slips of paper before the meditation**

Central altar should be covered with a red or black tablecloth and divided into 3 sections.

1. **Cauldron section**: Black candle, cauldron or cast iron pot, sterno, cooking tripod, plate or pie dish for under the sterno and tripod, wooden spoon, water, wine or milk, herbs and spices (whatever is on hand and feels right), raisins and/or nuts.

2. **Crossroads section:** White taper candle and candle holder (from which the tea-lights will be lighted), tea-lights, plate to hold the tea-lights; one for each participant.

3. **Rebirth section:** Vase with a large mouth and neck (as big as a large fist) , red candle and holder, frogs (optional), small crystal points or crystal beads, one for each participant.

Ritual Preparations - Central Altar

Cauldron section: The water in the cauldron (cast iron pot) should be hot. We usually boil the water first in a tea kettle and then pour it into the cauldron. Set the cauldron on the cooking tripod and light the sterno. Stir in the wine, herbs and spices before the circle starts. Keep the water hot to boiling during the circle. A steaming cauldron is an effective mood enhancer for the ritual. Light the candle. The raisins should be in plain view off to one side so the participants can easily reach them as they make their offerings. Keep the wooden spoon handy. Participants like to stir the "brew."

Crossroads section: Light the taper candle and arrange the unlit tea-lights on a plate. The participants will light tea-lights as part of the ritual.

Rebirth section: Wrap the vase in the black cloth with an opening at the mouth. Lay it on its side with the mouth facing the edge of the table. This will be Hecate's "womb." Put the crystal points or beads into the vase for the participants to withdraw as their "dream seed." Light the red candle and arrange the frogs around the womb.

Ritual Introduction:

(read or paraphrase the following)

Tonight's ritual will give you the opportunity to envision and call forth transformation. This can be in the form of something you want to release, or something you want to birth into your life, or a decision you need to make, for even a decision is the death of one possibility and the birth of another.

The central altar is divided into three sections, or smaller altars: the Cauldron, the Crossroads, and the Rebirth Altars.

Cauldron Altar: At the Cauldron Altar you are first invited to make an offering of gratitude to Hecate. Place some of the raisins into the cauldron while calling upon Hecate to assist you tonight and in the future as she both holds and guides you towards personal growth and transformation.

The cauldron represents the stage of death and endings. Here you may release into the cauldron that which no longer serves you. Place into the cauldron the slip of paper upon which you have written the symbolic word or phrase that represents that which you are ready to release. Take a moment to envision and feel it being released from your energy body.

Crossroads Altar: Circling to the right you will be at the Crossroads Altar. At this altar you are invited to light a candle to Hecate. Call upon Her for guidance on any decisions you need to make, or in formulating what you want to birth into your life.

Rebirth Altar: Circling to the right you will be at the Rebirth Altar. As you envision your rebirth you may withdraw from Hecate's womb a dream seed. Blow into the dream seed impregnating your dream with the breath of life, inspiration and motivation.

There is a sequence to approaching the different altars, but always feel free to take a moment to sit down if you need time to reflect before moving on to the next altar.

Ritual Invocations (Read or paraphrase as the first person approaches each altar during the ritual)

- ## Altar 1 The Cauldron of Transformation and Rebirth

Goddess Hecate, Wise Woman of the People, Crone of the Mysterious Underworld, Guardian of the Gates, Great One of Magic.

We stand in stillness behind all motion before your ancient cauldron of transformation and rebirth. We give unto you that which limits and weakens us, entangles us, binds us to disorder, blinds us to clarity, disorients us, and that which no longer serves our divine souls.

Receive our burdens into the dark depths of your bubbling cauldron; remove our attachments, purify them from our entanglements, decompose them to their bones, transform them and ready them for rebirth.

- ### Altar 2 The Crossroads:

Goddess Hecate, Hecate Trevia, Lady of the Three Ways, Goddess of the Roads, Protectress of the Journey, the One Who Lights the Way.

We stand before you at the crossroads of the past, present, and future, of the meeting point of heaven, earth, and the underworld. In this place of your domain we light candles in your name. We ask for guidance and clarity of vision for the best possible outcomes for the decisions that lay before us. We ask your help in shaping our dreams into the best possible forms for us at this time.

May your torchlight show us the way.

- **Altar 3 Rebirth**

Goddess Hecate, Heavenly Midwife to the Unborn, Keeper of the Gate Between Life and Death, Ancient Frog Goddess of Regeneration, Bringer of New Life Out of the Cauldron of Rebirth

We stand before the Gate of Rebirth and Transformation where you stir your cauldron of rebirth, spinning out threads of new life. Within the depths of your cauldron lie the fragile whispers of our dream-seeds, of decisions made with the clarity of your guidance, the weavings of a new path.

Smile upon our unborn dream-seeds, impart shape and form to them, give them the breath of life, and send them forth to be born into our lives. May your torch light the way for us. May your torch light the path before us, and may you guard us on our new journey.

If we have chosen wrongly, or if you have something better in store for us, send us messages loud and clear that we may re-shape our goals.

Closing Statement of Ritual (to be read when everyone has completed the ritual)

Goddess Hecate, Guardian of the Unconscious, Bringer of Light from the Darkness, Mistress of Magic, thank you for your presence and blessings tonight and always.
Blessed be.

HECATE
TABLE OF CORRESPONDENCES

Element: Earth

Symbols: Cauldron, crossroads, torchlight, three-headed statues or animals, trinity

Color: Black, orange, yellow-orange, red-orange

Animals: Frogs, dogs, owls, bats, snakes, boars

Companions: Three headed dog, Cerberus

Moon: Dark of the moon

Geography: Ancient Thrace - present day Greece and Bulgaria

Timeframe: Pre-Hellenic to 3rd or 4th Century CE Greece

Rocks/Crystals: Moonstone, black tourmaline, black onyx, hematite, smoky quartz, silver

Plants: Willow, dark yew, blackthorn, groves of trees, mugwort, myrrh, cinnamon

Foods: Raisin and currant cakes, wine, milk, honey

In Her Name Circle Program

(The following is a proposed agenda if you choose to hold a circle to celebrate Hecate)

Intro: (10 min) Name, city, word of their emotion at the moment

Casting the Circle: (3min)

Talk: Hecate – (25 min)

Q&A: **(**10 min**)**

Guided Visualization: Hecate at the Crossroads - (15 min)

> **Music   Suggestion:** "Transformation"   – *Return* by Sophia, Chakra Healing Zone

Individual Process – Journaling and/or drawing – writing what they want to release on the slips of paper (5 min)

Group Share: (5 to 10 min)

Ritual: Release and Rebirth (25min)

> **Music Suggestion:** "Hecate" – *The Year is a Dancing Woman*, Vol. 2 by Ruth Barrett

Group Share (10 min)

Goddess Cards (10 min)

Closing: (2 min)

    Releasing the Directions – (3min)

    Total time: 2 hrs.

ABOUT THE AUTHOR

Joy F. Reichard, M.A., is an Amazon Bestselling Author of *Celebrate the Divine Feminine: Reclaim Your Power with Ancient Goddess Wisdom*, the e-book *52 Weeks of the Divine Feminine,* as well as numerous e-books on various Divine Feminine Archetypes. With a Master's Degree in Women's Spirituality, Joy has led classes, workshops, and sacred women's circles since 2005.

Today Joy continues to use the mythology and legends of the Sacred Feminine as teaching stories helping women in their healing, transformation, and empowerment. Joy is the creator of "In Her Name Circles" which honors feminine wisdom and focuses on woman's spiritual and personal growth. In 2014 Joy launched "Persephone's Journey; A Wisdom School for Awakening Women." The schedule of her current classes can be found at **http://joyreichard.com/workshops/persephones-journey-school-for-awakening-women/**

Based in San Mateo, CA, Joy Reichard has a private practice as a transformational life coach, clinical hypnotherapist, and spiritual counselor helping visionary women and men who hear their soul's call to live their full potential and find greater joy and fulfillment.

More information on Joy Reichard can be found at **http://.healingwithjoy.net** and http://celebratedivinefeminine.com

Made in the USA
San Bernardino, CA
26 February 2017